Church Basics

Understanding the
Great Commission

Series Editor Jonathan Leeman
Author Mark Dever

PUBLISHING GROUP
Nashville, Tennessee

978-1-4336-8894-2

Published by B&H Publishing Group
Nashville, Tennessee

Dewey Decimal Classification: 260
Subject Heading: CHURCH \ EVANGELISTIC WORK \
CHRISTIAN MISSIONS

1 2 3 4 5 6 7 8 • 20 19 18 17 16

CONTENTS

CHURCH BASICS SERIES PREFACE

The Christian life is the churched life. This basic biblical conviction informs every book in the Church Basics series.

That conviction in turn affects how each author treats his topic. For instance, the Lord's Supper is not a private, mystical act between you and Jesus. It is a meal around the family table in which you commune with Christ and Christ's people. The Great Commission is not a license to head into the nations as Jesus' witness all by oneself. It is a charge given to the whole church to be fulfilled by the whole church. The authority of the church rests not only with the leaders, but with the entire assembly. Every member has a job to do, including you.

Every book is written *for* the average church member, and this is a crucial point. If the Christian life is a churched life, then you, a baptized believer and church member, have a responsibility to understand these basic topics. Just as Jesus charges you with promoting and protecting his gospel message, so he charges you with promoting and protecting his gospel people, the church. These books will explain how.

You are like a shareholder in Christ's gospel ministry corporation. And what do good shareholders do? They study their company, study the market, and study the competition. They want the most out of their investment. You, Christian, have invested your whole life in the gospel. The purpose of the series, then, is to help you maximize the health and kingdom profitability of your local congregation for God's glorious gospel ends.

Are you ready to get to work?

Jonathan Leeman
Series Editor

Books in the Church Basics series:

CHAPTER 1

The Great Commission, You, and the Local Church

One way to describe the goal of this book is to help you understand the Great Commission and what it means in your individual Christian life.

The Bible does not use the words "Great Commission," but Christians have long used this phrase to describe the final glorious command that Jesus gave before ascending into heaven. Do you remember it? Here it is:

> Then Jesus came near and said to them, "All authority has been given to Me in heaven and on earth. Go, therefore, and make disciples of all nations, baptizing them in the name of the Father and of the Son and of the Holy Spirit, teaching them to observe everything I have commanded you. And remember, I am with you always, to the end of the age." (Matt. 28:18–20)

During his ministry before the crucifixion, Jesus had said that his mission was only to the lost sheep of Israel (Matt. 15:24). But now, after the resurrection, he is the exalted judge of all the earth. He rose with the authority of the Almighty, like the Son of Man mentioned in Daniel 7. Jesus' rule extends beyond Israel to all nations. He has *all* authority in heaven and earth.

After asserting this authority, Jesus tells his disciples to make disciples. Grammatically, this is the one imperative verb in the original

Greek: make disciples. And that command is surrounded by three participles, so that we could translate the verbal phrases like this:

Going, *make disciples,* baptizing and teaching.

The first participle—*going*—is usually translated "go." This is not a bad thing because it is the first word in the sentence and it occurs before "make disciples." Greek readers would have understood that it should receive special emphasis. It's fine then for us to translate it as "go."

But if making disciples depends on going, baptizing, and teaching, who is sending the goers? And who is doing the baptizing and teaching? Is this work accomplished primarily through individual evangelizing and discipling? Or some other way?

Churches Fulfilling the Great Commission Through Planting Churches

When I look at books on the Great Commission, I find they often focus on evangelism or missions. They emphasize what we as Christians do individually. And I wrote one such book. It's called *The Gospel and Personal Evangelism.* I hope you will read it! Certainly the Great Commission cannot be fulfilled without individuals sharing the gospel and teaching others. But is that all there is to the Great Commission— individual Christians holding plane tickets and gospel tracts in their hands? Or do Jesus' words imply anything else?

That brings us to the second way to describe the purpose of this book: I hope to help you see that the Great Commission is normally fulfilled through planting and growing local churches. Churches fulfill the Great Commission through planting more churches. So the Great Commission involves you, the individual Christian. But the Great Commission also involves you *through* your local church. That is the normal way God means for us to go, make disciples, baptize, and teach.

God's Promise to Abraham and to Us

Do you remember what God promised to Isaiah about the Messiah centuries before Jesus gave this commission? God said, "It is not enough for you to be My Servant raising up the tribes of Jacob and restoring the protected ones of Israel. I will also make you a light for the nations, to be My salvation to the ends of the earth" (Isa. 49:6).

The very first verse of Matthew's Gospel invokes this ancient promise to Isaiah by going back further still—to Abraham. Matthew 1:1 calls Jesus the "Son of Abraham," reminding us of God's original promise to Abraham: "I will make you into a great nation" and "all the peoples on earth will be blessed through you" (Gen. 12:2–3).

In other words, the Bible's testimony is consistent: God has always had a plan to bring his salvation to the ends of the earth—to all nations and all peoples.

Now, in the last verses of Matthew's Gospel, we find these gathered disciples standing on a mountain with Jesus, learning that God's promise of international blessing to Abraham culminated here. Here is how God would fulfill his promise to Abraham. Here is how all nations on earth would be blessed. *All* the disciples would be responsible to ensure that the message of the gospel would go to *all* nations, and *all* disciples of Jesus Christ would be called to obey *all* the commandments of Jesus. For this great enterprise, Jesus promised them that he, who now possessed *all* authority, would be with them *all* their days, until he returns.

Was this just a promise for the first apostles? No. Jesus knew that the apostles' lives would end long before his return.

Rather, Jesus promised that he would be with them until the end of the age so that we would know that this promise is for us, too. Jesus knew he would continue working generation after generation long after this first group was gone. We, too, receive the promise of Christ's presence.

This commission is for us!

What Is a Church?

And it's not just for us as individual Christians. It is for us as churches and church members.

What is a church? It is a body of Christians who are in regular and accountable fellowship, where the Word is rightly preached, and baptism and the Lord's Supper are rightly administered.

Let me unpack that. First, a church is a place where God's Word is rightly preached. After all, we are saved by the preaching of God's Word. God creates his people through his Word: "So faith comes from what is heard, and what is heard comes through the message about Christ" (Rom. 10:17). It is as if the whole world is walking along. Then someone speaks God's promises, a group of people look up, turn, and start walking in the direction of those promises. They hear them and believe them. The preached Word is foundational to a church.

But second, a church is a place where the ordinances are rightly practiced. After all, the ordinances mark off a church. The ordinances don't save us. They are signs of the gospel and what we use to affirm one another as belonging to the gospel. They are how the fellowship of the church exercises its accountability among one another. (See Bobby Jamieson's two books in the Church Basics series: *Understanding Baptism* and *Understanding the Lord's Supper*.)

People sometimes say that the church is a people, not a place. In fact, a kind of place is necessary: you need a gathering of believers. And then you need the preaching of the Word and the administering of the ordinances in that gathering to make it a church as opposed to any other gathering of Christians. The Word creates us as Christ's people, and the ordinances mark us off.

So think once more of the four commands of the Great Commission: go, make disciples, baptize, and teach. Who does all this? Who sends out the going Christians to make disciples? The local church. And who names them as disciples by baptizing them, and then helps them to grow by teaching them? The local church does.

The local church is the normal means God has given us to fulfill the Great Commission. That's the message of this book.

Is This Book for You?

Who then is the intended audience for this book? It is for every believer, maybe especially the young believer. I will walk you through the Bible, especially in the early chapters, and try to provide you with some basic building blocks for how you understand your Christianity in relation to the Great Commission and your church.

Some of the lessons, particularly in the later chapters, might feel more relevant to church leaders. But even if it's the leaders who have a firmer hand on the programmatic levers in a church's life, ultimately it is the saints who need to understand what Jesus means when he says go, make disciples, baptize, and teach. He gives the commission to all of us. To you. You need to share Jesus' vision. Do you?

CHAPTER 2

God's Word, God's People

Many people claim to love God, and even to have a relationship with him. And yet they have no interest in his Word, which are the sixty-six books of the Old and New Testament. But what do you think my wife would say if I claimed to love her, but showed absolutely no interest in her words?

You can gauge a person's love for God by his or her love for God's Word. In fact, that's the difference between God's people and the world: God's people, throughout the Bible, gather around God's Word. They listen for it, they obey it, they love it (see Psalm 119!).

In the last chapter, I concluded by pulling in the magnifying glass on a local church. A local church, I said, is a gathering of people where God's Word is rightly preached and the ordinances are rightly administered.

Now I want to pull way back and look at the Bible as a whole, from beginning to end. What we find is that the whole Bible focuses on God revealing himself through his Word and doing so in order to call a people to himself.

God's Word

God wants himself to be known, and he wants a people to trust him. That is the point of the Old and New Testaments. God makes promises, God keeps promises, and we are to respond in trust.

It is God's gospel Word, we saw in chapter 1, which saves and creates God's people. The gospel is "the power of God for the salvation of everyone who believes," says Paul (Rom. 1:16 NIV).

So God's Word comes, and it comes with a challenge: will you believe it and trust God with your whole life?

This is the challenge posed throughout Scripture. God revealed himself by speaking to Adam, then Noah, then Abraham, then Moses. And God commends the person who, like Abraham, hears his Word and believes it (see Rom. 4); who acts on it.

Or think of wisdom in the book of Proverbs. The wisdom of God comes, holds out truth, and invites us to believe, accept, and act on the Word. Will we respond like the wise son or the foolish son?

So God gives his Word and his promises to us, and we are to respond by trusting his Word and believing his promises. Adam and Eve failed to trust and believe in the garden of Eden. Jesus trusted and believed perfectly throughout his life, even in the garden of Gethsemane. We, too, can begin to have the relationship with God for which we were made by hearing and believing God's Word.

This is fundamental to being a Christian. The Bible teaches that we have all disobeyed God's Word and ignored his commandments. And since he is a good God, he will punish our sin. Our only hope to escape his punishment is not to reform our lives, because that wouldn't do anything about the sins we've already committed. We must have a Savior and a substitute—someone who will bear God's punishment for us. And that's what the Lord Jesus has done. He lived a life of complete trust in God's Word and instruction. And he died on the cross bearing the punishment for all who would turn from their sins and trust in him and his Word.

God's People

The question is, whom does God mean to save to himself? Does he mean merely to save disconnected individuals? No, he means to save a people.

At the beginning of the Bible, God makes Adam individually in his own image. But God also follows the pattern—beginning in these first chapters—of creating a people. So he makes not just Adam, but Adam and Eve, and there is something of God's image displayed in Adam and Eve together, as well as in the family they create.

The pattern continues. It's Noah and his family that are saved; Abram and his family who are called; the nation of Israel who is set apart throughout the whole Old Testament. God works not just with individuals, but with the people of Israel.

The corporate pattern makes sense. Something of God's character can be made known and displayed only through the interactions of people with each other. Consider the fruit of the Spirit in Galatians 5: love, joy, peace, patience, kindness, goodness, faith, gentleness, self-control. How many of those could you practice living by yourself on an island? Maybe a few of them? But really such qualities can only be displayed in how people interact with one another.

Most crucially, what distinguishes God's people from the world is that God's people listen to God's voice and gather around his Word. Noah listens to God when commanded to build an ark. Abraham hears God's word and follows God to a new land. The people of Israel were to be set apart from the nations by their obedience to what the Bible calls God's ten words, or the Ten Commandments.

The same story is true in the New Testament. We will look at the Gospels and the Epistles in the coming chapters. For now, let's jump to Revelation and the end of the Bible. There we discover that Matthew 28 is fulfilled in the great heavenly church. If you are a Christian, one day you will stand in this heavenly assembly of which the apostle John was given a glimpse:

After this I looked, and there was a vast multitude from
every nation, tribe, people, and language, which no one could
number, standing before the throne and before the Lamb. They
were robed in white with palm branches in their hands. And
they cried out in a loud voice:
Salvation belongs to our God, who is seated on the throne,
and to the Lamb! (Rev. 7:9–10)

Here we have a multitude of people from all over the world testify-
ing to the faithfulness of God forever. These are the people who have
believed in God's Word. Some have been persecuted "because of God's
Word" (Rev. 6:9; 20:4). And Jesus himself is described as the Word of
God (Rev. 19:13). This assembly is what we are headed toward! How
wonderful to know that the Great Commission *will* work!

God will have a community who knows him and praises him as
God. This is the big picture of the Bible. It begins with God revealing
himself through his words, and it concludes with a people who know
him, trust him, and praise him.

Back to the Church and the Commission

Suppose we zoom the camera from its wide-angle lens on all
of Scripture back to the local church. What do we find? That question takes us into the next few chapters. But remember what we said
a church is. It's a gathering of people, built upon their shared trust
in God's Word. It's a presentation—a foreshadowing—of that great
assembly in Revelation. Any one local gathering doesn't feature every
nation, tribe, people, and language like that end time assembly. But
they are beginning to. We see the firstfruits. Winter has passed, and
the spring buds on the tree have begun to appear. Just wait and see!

The Great Commission, furthermore, calls us to herald God's
Word to the nations and gather his people. It calls us to *make disciples*
of the nations so that they, too, would believe and come in.

CHAPTER 3

Heaven's Love, Heaven's Truth, Heaven's People

I have been a pastor in Washington, DC, for more than two decades. How many elections cycles is that? More than a few generals and journalists, senators and Hill staffers, have come and gone since I first arrived.

It is not uncommon for young people to show up with grand visions of the changes they can make. And Christians in politics should fight for good changes. It is one way to love our neighbors. The trouble comes when people try to use the mechanisms of the state—the power of the sword—to bring heaven to earth. If cynicism more often characterizes the older generations in politics, utopianism is the more common temptation among the younger. Aside from the fact that utopianism has been the source of some of history's greatest atrocities, it fundamentally misunderstands God's plans for history. Nothing in the New Testament teaches us to expect that Christ's kingdom shall come, and that his will shall ultimately be done on earth as it is in heaven, thanks to the work of presidents or prime ministers.

But there is one place we should look for the firstfruits of heaven on earth. Remember how I concluded chapter 2? The local church, I said, is a presentation of that great assembly in Revelation. It's where we catch the first glimpses of heaven's springtime blossoms.

In the last chapter, we jumped from the Old Testament straight to the final glorious assembly gathered from every nation, tribe, and language in the book of Revelation, skipping clean over the Gospels, Acts, and the Epistles. That needs to be addressed.

We start with Jesus. How does Jesus regard the church? And what does Jesus call the church to do and to be? Jesus loves the church entirely. And just as Jesus represents heaven on earth, so he calls the church to do the same.

Jesus' Love for the Church

Jesus loved the church to the end. That's what John said right before Jesus washed the disciples' feet, symbolizing the more permanent washing he was about to accomplish through his death: "Having loved His own who were in the world, He loved them to the end" (John 13:1).

Jesus purchased the church with his own blood (Acts 20:28).

Jesus founded the church (Matt. 16:18).

Jesus addresses, instructs, and shows his love for churches in both encouragement and warning (Rev. 2—3).

Jesus' love for the church, in fact, provides the model by which husbands are to love their wives. Says Paul:

> Husbands, love your wives, just as Christ loved the church
> and gave Himself for her to make her holy, cleansing her with
> the washing of water by the word. He did this to present the
> church to Himself in splendor, without spot or wrinkle or
> anything like that, but holy and blameless. In the same way,
> husbands are to love their wives as their own bodies. He who
> loves his wife loves himself. For no one ever hates his own flesh
> but provides and cares for it, just as Christ does for the church,
> since we are members of His body. For this reason a man will
> leave his father and mother and be joined to his wife, and the
> two will become one flesh. This mystery is profound, but I am
> talking about Christ and the church. To sum up, each one of

you is to love his wife as himself, and the wife is to respect her husband. (Eph. 5:25–33)

Christ gave himself for the church. He seeks its holiness. He cleanses it with the Word. He provides and cares for the church. He loves it as his own body.

Demonstrating Heaven's Love

So much does Jesus love the church that he means to identify it with himself. Among other things, this means that our love for one another in the church should look like his love. "I give you a new command," said Jesus, "Love one another. Just as I have loved you, you must also love one another. By this all people will know that you are My disciples, if you have love for one another" (John 13:34–35). The church is to demonstrate heaven's own love. Such one-another love is a distinctive of Christ's disciples. By it the nations will know that we belong to him.

But it's not just other Christians that we should love. We demonstrate God's love for the world in our love for outsiders too. Jesus connects loving one's neighbor with loving God. "Which command is the most important of all?" asked the scribe. Jesus answered, "Love the Lord your God with all your heart, soul, mind, and strength. And love your neighbor as yourselves" (Mark 12:28–31). The claim to love God brings a necessary horizontal element. You can have wonderfully rich quiet times, but if that doesn't translate into how you treat other people, then something is wrong. The normal, natural way for Christians to express our love to God is not merely in singing hymns to him, though that is wonderful. It is also in giving ourselves in love to others.

Churches should be centers for such loving activity. It's where heaven's love shows up, first in the pronouncement of Christ's love for us in the gospel, and second in our love for insiders and outsiders alike.

Recognizing Heaven's Truths and Heaven's People

Since Jesus means to identify these people with himself, and since he wants their love for one another to represent his love for them, it's not surprising that he wants them marked off with his name. He wants them formally recognized as belonging to him.

This is why Jesus, in the Great Commission, commands all disciples to be baptized into the name of the Father and of the Son and of the Spirit, and why the book of Acts refers again and again to being baptized into Jesus' name. It is as if Christ wants us to wear the nametag that has his name on it! He wants the nations to identify us with him.

And remember, this is the one who has received all authority in heaven and on earth. What on earth could the disciples have thought when they heard him say this! We are to be named together with the one who bears God's own authority?

It's important not to read the command to baptize in isolation, as Christians so often do. Rather, we should read it together with Matthew 16 and 18, where Jesus had already given responsibility and authority first to the apostles and then to local churches. Who has the authority to baptize and identify people with Christ? In ordinary circumstances, it's the church.

In Matthew 16:16, Peter professes that Jesus is the Christ, the Son of the living God, to which Jesus responds,

> Simon son of Jonah, you are blessed because flesh and blood
> did not reveal this to you, but My Father in heaven. And I also
> say to you that you are Peter, and on this rock I will build My
> church, and the forces of Hades will not overpower it. I will
> give you the keys of the kingdom of heaven, and whatever you
> bind on earth is already bound in heaven, and whatever you
> loose on earth is already loosed in heaven. (vv. 17–19)

On behalf of the Father in heaven, Jesus affirms Peter and Peter's answer. Then he gives the keys of the kingdom to make these same kinds of recognitions on behalf of heaven. Peter and the apostles would possess heaven's authority to affirm confessions and confessors of the gospel, like Jesus did with Peter.

More remarkable still, Jesus then gives this same authority to the local church in chapter 18. If a person claiming to be a Christian has been confronted several times over unrepentant sin, Jesus concludes that the church should assess the man, and then treat him as an outsider if he remains unrepentant:

> But if he doesn't pay attention even to the church, let him
> be like an unbeliever and a tax collector to you. I assure you:
> Whatever you bind on earth is already bound in heaven,
> and whatever you loose on earth is already loosed in heaven.
> (18:17–18)

The church possesses the authority to treat him like an unbeliever by virtue of the fact that it possesses the keys of binding and loosing. Just as the keys can be used to recognize a true gospel confession and confessor, so they can be used to deny a false gospel confession and confessor.

Why would I say that, ordinarily, local churches possess the authority to baptize? Because Matthew 16 and 18 tell us that local churches possess Christ's keys. They possess the authority to affirm or recognize right confessions and confessors, as Jesus did with Peter. And they have the authority to deny them, as Jesus instructs the church to do in instances of church discipline. Jesus concludes chapter 18's episode by explaining, "For where two or three are gathered together in My name, I am there among them" (v. 20). Who has authority to baptize in Jesus' name? It is the people who gather in his name. Jesus abides there, says chapter 18; and he will abide there till the end, says chapter 28. (For more on these chapters and the keys of the kingdom, see Jonathan Leeman's *Understanding the Congregation's Authority* in the Church Basics series.)

To sum all this up, churches possess the authority to recognize heaven's truth and to recognize heaven's people, just as they should demonstrate heaven's love.

God's Commitment to Church Planting

Christ loves the church. And when he ascended to heaven he sent the Spirit who has given gifts to the church, which build it up. Father, Son, and Holy Spirit are committed to the church. Father, Son, and Spirit are committed to planting churches.

The church is not fundamentally a human idea, or a human creation. Fundamentally, it is God's idea and God's work. In one sense, God is the great church planter! He has commissioned the disciples to gather in his name, baptize in his name, teach in his name.

So when you're involved in a church, you don't have to wonder if it will ultimately work. Christ has promised that the gates of Hades will not prevail against the church. Christ has promised that he will have a witness to himself when he returns.

CHAPTER 4

Preach the Gospel, Gather a Church

Does Jesus intend for churches to work like the Department of Motor Vehicles (DMV), but for the Christian life?

When the DMV gives you a driver's license, you have the ability to drive wherever you want. They give you the responsibility, and then you are on your own. There are no weekly gatherings of people with driver's licenses. There is no need to know the names of other licensees or to care for one another. There are no driver-license pastors or shepherds, whose work is to make sure you are growing in your understanding of motor vehicle safety.

Strangely, this is how some Christians hear Jesus' Great Commission: "Go, make disciples, baptize, and teach" somehow becomes "Make converts, give them the license of baptism, and then let them go!" Sure, maybe people should check in on the church once in a while, like getting your license renewed every few years. And they should keep reading their Bibles and learning. But it's really all up to them now.

There are a number of things we might say in response to the DMV version of the Great Commission. First, it ignores what the apostles actually did after Jesus ascended. Second, it ignores what the Commission says about teaching. Third, it ignores what the Commission says about obeying. There you have the plan for this chapter and the next two!

Where the Gospel Goes, Churches Show Up

Did the apostles primarily fulfill the Great Commission through individual evangelizing and discipling only? The command to "make disciples" certainly involves telling the message. But how did the apostles do it?

Consider the story of the gospel's spread in the book of Acts. It turns out that the story of gospel's spread is the story of the spread of churches. It all begins in Jerusalem and then the story moves outward: wherever the gospel goes, churches show up.

- In chapter 2, Peter preaches a message of repentance and forgiveness of sins. And "those who accepted his message were baptized, and that day about 3,000 people were added to them" (v. 41). Notice, new disciples were added to *something*. Added to what? The church in Jerusalem (see 5:11; 8:1).

- In chapter 11, we learn that those scattered by the persecution in Jerusalem went to Antioch "proclaiming the good news about the Lord Jesus" (v. 20), and a "large number who believed turned to the Lord" (v. 21). The church in Jerusalem then sent Barnabas to Antioch to help with the planting project. More disciples "were added" (v. 24). Barnabas recruits Paul, and "for a whole year they met with the church and taught large numbers" (v. 26).

- In chapter 14, Paul and Barnabas visit Iconium "and spoke in such a way that a great number of both Jews and Greeks believed" (v. 1). Then they went to Lystra "and kept evangelizing" (v. 7). Nowhere does the text say, "And so they started a church." But that's exactly what happened. Half a chapter later, Paul and Barnabas "returned to Lystra, to Iconium, and to Antioch" (v. 21), and this time "they appointed elders in every church" (v. 23). Believers gathered together in churches.

- In chapter 18, the Corinthian church was planted when many heard, believed, and were baptized (v. 8).

- In chapter 19, Paul preaches in Ephesus and many are converted. Again, the text never explicitly says, "and they planted a church," but by the time we get to chapter 20, we know that's exactly what happened: Paul "sent to Ephesus and called for the elders of the church" (v. 17).
- The book of Acts concludes with Paul preaching in Rome, and of course there is eventually a church (or churches) in Rome, as the letter to the Romans attests (see Rom. 1:7; 16:5).

What did the apostles do? They preached and gathered churches. Churches are at the center of God's Great Commission plan.

Prominent on Stage

Maybe you've never read the book of Acts like this. Maybe you've only seen individual acts of heroism and faith. But read Acts again and notice how prominent on stage the local church is (emphasis added below). Who sends out the apostles and other delegates? The local church.

- "Then the report about them was heard by the church that was at Jerusalem, and *they sent out* Barnabas to travel as far as Antioch" (11:22).
- "When they had been *sent on their way by the church* . . ." (15:3).

To whom do these delegates come back and report? The local church.

- "After they arrived and *gathered the church together*, they reported everything God had done with them and that He had opened the door of faith to the Gentiles" (14:27; also, 16:4–5).
- "When they arrived at Jerusalem, they were *welcomed by the church*, the apostles, and the elders" (15:4).

Who's making decisions? The local church.

- "The proposal pleased the whole company. So *they chose* . . ." (6:5).

- "Then the apostles and the elders, *with the whole church, decided to select* men who were among them and to send them to Antioch" (15:22).

What does God do? He provides elders for the local church.

- "When they had *appointed elders in every church* and prayed with fasting, they committed them to the Lord in whom they had believed" (14:23).
- "Be on guard for yourselves and for all the flock that the Holy Spirit has *appointed you to as overseers,* to shepherd the church of God" (20:28).

The whole book of Acts centers around not just individual evangelizing and discipling, but evangelizing and discipling in the context of the local church. The story of the spread of the gospel is the story of local churches.

Not Just Acts

Of course, the church is a prominent actor on stage not only in the book of Acts. It plays a lead role throughout the New Testament. The majority of the New Testament letters are addressed to churches: "To God's church at Corinth" (1 Cor. 1:2); "To the churches of Galatia" (Gal. 1:2); "To all the saints in Christ Jesus who are in Philippi, including the overseers and deacons" (Phil. 1:1); "To the church of the Thessalonians" (1 Thess. 1:1).

The churches greet and thank one another: "Not only do I thank them, but so do all the Gentile churches" (Rom. 16:4); "All the churches of Christ send you greetings" (Rom. 16:16); "The churches of Asia greet you" (1 Cor. 16:19).

The apostles assume and command the Christians to gather as churches for teaching, the Lord's Supper, and mutual encouragement:

- ". . . just as I teach everywhere in every church" (1 Cor. 4:17; also 7:17).
- "I hear that when you come together as a church there are divisions among you. . . . Therefore, my brothers, when you come together to eat, wait for one another" (1 Cor. 11:18, 33).
- "When this letter has been read among you, have it read also in the church of the Laodiceans; and see that you also read the letter from Laodicea" (Col. 4:16).
- "And let us be concerned about one another in order to promote love and good works, not staying away from our worship meetings, as some habitually do, but encouraging each other, and all the more as you see the day drawing near" (Heb. 10:24–25).

The churches show concern for one another:

- "[Titus] was also appointed by the churches to accompany us with this gift that is being administered by us" (2 Cor. 8:19);
- "Now about the collection for the saints: You should do the same as I instructed the Galatian churches. On the first day of the week, each of you is to set something aside. . . . When I arrive, I will send with letters those you recommend to carry your gracious gift to Jerusalem" (1 Cor. 16:1–3).

The churches send missionaries and work to plant other churches:

- "As for our brothers, they are the messengers of the churches" (2 Cor. 8:23).
- "When I left Macedonia, no church shared with me in the matter of giving and receiving except you alone" (Phil. 4:15).
- "You will do well to send them on their journey in a manner worthy of God, since they set out for the sake of the Name, accepting nothing from pagans. Therefore, we ought to support such men so that we can be coworkers with the truth" (3 John 6–8).

Paul expresses his care for Christians as "my care for all the churches" (2 Cor. 11:28). New Testament commentator Peter O'Brien observes that Paul's "ambition to preach the gospel where Christ was not acknowledged as Lord, in order not to build on another's foundation . . . is evidence that primary evangelism was integral to his missionary commission." But that was not the only element in Paul's commission. O'Brien continues: "Paul's work was not finished until he had instructed the Christians and left a mature and settled congregation."[1]

The Missionary Task: Proclaiming Then Gathering

There are many examples I could use. The point is, in the New Testament, the Christian life is the churched life. Our discipleship to Christ occurs in and through churches.

What that means is, the missionary mandate is not complete until new believers are settled in local congregations. O'Brien offers a wonderful summary of how Paul understood the Christian's basic commission:

> Paul not only proclaimed the gospel and, under God, converted men and women. He also founded churches as a necessary element in his missionary task. Conversion to Christ meant incorporation into him, and thus membership within a Christian community. . . . it is clear that the nurture of emerging churches is understood by Paul to be "an integral feature of his missionary task."[2]

Christians and even church leaders today might treat the local church like an office of the DMV. They might read the Great Commission as saying, "Give them their licenses and let them go!" But that is not how the apostles viewed their work. They preached the gospel and planted churches. The early churches did the same.

CHAPTER 5

Teaching with Correction and Oversight

A local church is not the DMV who issues licenses through baptism. That was the point of the last chapter. Yet just as we don't want a "DMV version" of the Great Commission, we don't want an "information booth" version. The local church is not an information booth!

Maybe this sounds silly to say. No one says the church is an information booth. But many Christians do treat the church like a preaching station. They show up on Sunday, receive a download of information, and then spend the rest of the week better informed, yes, but scarcely connected to the other members of the church or the pastors. That's how an information booth works. You walk up to the desk, ask your question, and walk away better informed. But you leave with no relational ties to the people back at the desk. They've performed their duty, and now you can get on with your business.

Certainly, the Great Commission commands churches to teach. Remember what it says? Go and make disciples . . . *teaching*. And that's what I want to talk about now. But notice how the commission couples baptizing and teaching: go and make disciples, *baptizing and teaching*. The text envisions teaching being done in the context of accountability, oversight, and the correct administration of the ordinances.

We see this in the book of Matthew. We see this in the rest of the New Testament.

Briefly Back to Matthew

Think back to our earlier discussion of Matthew. In chapter 28, Jesus commands the disciples to baptize new disciples into the name of the Father, Son, and Spirit. These are people who make professions of faith in Jesus as the Messiah who died for sin and was raised again.

But what happens when someone talks the talk but does not walk the walk? One professes trust in Christ, but then doesn't repent of some sin? Jesus answered that question for us back in Matthew 18. The church of at least two or three, which gathers in Jesus' name, should exercise the keys and remove the individual from membership in the church.

Now go back to Matthew 28. When Jesus commands the disciples to teach, does he have something like an information booth in mind? Or even a seminary chapel lecture? No! These disciples are both baptized and taught. A church gives them a Jesus nametag, but then it keeps watch on the individual to make sure he or she does not end up in a Matthew 18 situation.

The underlying lesson here is, new believers are ordinarily baptized into church membership, where the teaching occurs. Exceptions exist. You might think of Philip and the Ethiopian eunuch in Acts 8. But the situation in Acts 2 is more typical. Peter preaches the gospel. His hearers are cut to the heart and ask what they must do to be saved (v. 37). Peter says, "Repent and be baptized" (v. 38). Then Luke, the author, observes, "So those who accepted his message were baptized, and that day about 3,000 people were added to them" (v. 41). The people are baptized into membership of the Jerusalem church, where they are taught: "And they devoted themselves to the apostles' teaching . . ." (v. 42).

Shepherds: Teaching + Overseeing

The manner in which the rest of the New Testament talks about teaching reinforces the idea that the Great Commission's command to teach envisions church planting. You can see this in the fact that churches are given shepherds to teach them. They are not given lecturers. They are not given podcast preachers or information booth attendants. They are given shepherds, who combine both teaching and overseeing.

The shepherds guard the sheep (Acts 20:28–31; 1 Pet. 5:1–5; 2 Tim. 4:2). The shepherds guide the sheep (1 Thess. 5:12). The shepherds feed and equip the sheep (John 21:15–17; Eph. 4:11–16). The shepherds guard the gospel (1 Cor. 15:1–3; 1 Tim. 1:18–19).

Paul's charge to the Ephesians elders illustrates this well. "I did not shrink back from declaring to you the whole plan of God," he says. Then he exhorts them, "Be on guard for yourselves and for all the flock that the Holy Spirit has appointed you to as overseers, to shepherd the church of God" (Acts 20:27–28). An elder must do straight Bible teaching. That's critical. So Paul preaches the whole plan of God. But a lecturer, podcast preacher, or man standing at an information booth can declare the whole plan of God. Paul has something more personal and involved and accountability-creating in mind. These elders should teach the Bible, but as they do they guard and shepherd the particular flock that the Holy Spirit has given them.

God did not design the Christian life to be lived out by ourselves; that's why he has given us shepherds. The shepherd is more than a "teacher." He is an overseer too. And this makes sense! A sheep that's converted should not hang out by himself. We live in a fallen, wolfy world (see Acts 20:29–30)! A sheep needs to get himself into a flock where there are shepherds who will guard him. It's a proud and stupid thing for a sheep to remain by himself, as if there were no wolves.

Members: Speaking Truth to One Another

The duty of sheep to care for and instruct one another also reinforces the idea that teaching should occur primarily in the context of a local church and its accountability. The whole congregation should be involved in sanctifying and protecting one another. Jesus instructs one member to be forthright with another member when there is an offense between them (Matt. 18:15). Paul exhorts, "Let the message about the Messiah dwell richly among you, teaching and admonishing one another" (Col. 3:16). Elsewhere he instructs, "Speak the truth, each one to his neighbor, because we are members of one another" (Eph. 4:25), and we should speak only "what is good for building up someone in need, so that it gives grace to those who hear" (v. 29). The sheep help feed each other (1 Cor. 12; 14), and they help to guard the gospel in a church (Gal. 1:6–9; negative example in 2 Tim. 4:3).

No single sheep will be perfectly discerning. We need one another. That's why it takes a church, with faithful elders and a faithful congregation working together, to protect the gospel. How do scattered Christians, unaccountable to anyone but themselves, protect the gospel? The church is the pillar and foundation of truth (1 Tim. 3:15).

CHAPTER 6

Membership and a Self-Conscious Commitment

If you come to join the church where I pastor, one of the other pastors or I will do a membership interview with you. I will start with basic questions about your physical address, what you do, whether you have a spouse and children. But pretty quickly I will ask how you became a Christian. At the conclusion of this, I will ask you to explain the gospel in sixty seconds or less.

Here I am looking for you to present a basic acquaintance with what the gospel says about God, about man, about Christ, and about the necessary response. God is good and created us good. But we sinned against God and earned his just wrath. Christ therefore came, lived the perfect life we should have lived, and died the shameful death we should die. He took God's punishment for sin on himself as a substitute, and then rose again defeating sin and death. He now offers salvation to all who repent and believe.

If you leave something out, I will ask a question or two to clarify. Sometimes people mention that Jesus died on the cross for the forgiveness of sin, but they forget the resurrection! A quick question clears that up: "Did he remain in the grave?" "Oh no!"

More often, people fail to say anything about repentance. So I might ask something like this: "Suppose you have a friend who calls himself a Christian, but he is living with his girlfriend. What would you say?" I'm hoping they will say that a person should not call himself or herself a Christian and yet live in unrepentant sin.

Jesus wants disciples, not merely decisions. He wants people whose lives are fashioned and shaped by the teaching of Scripture.

Take a look again at the final command in Matthew 28: Go and make disciples, baptizing and "teaching them everything I have commanded you." Is that what it says? No. Jesus' final command to his disciples in Matthew's gospel is this: "teaching them *to obey* everything I have commanded you" (v. 20 NIV).

The Great Commission tasks churches with teaching the commands of Jesus, and with teaching people to obey his commands. Becoming a disciple, we can therefore say on the flip side, involves obeying and committing oneself to obedience. Are there any true Christians who don't commit themselves to obedience? No.

To this end of making disciples—not one-time-decision-makers— the apostles spread the gospel by planting churches, churches that teach and provide the accountability-structure (through baptism) inside of which teaching occurs. Becoming a disciple, then, involves self-consciously committing to obeying Scripture and to the accountability structure of a church.

This brings us to the topic of church membership.

The Membership Triangle

I often explain biblical church membership with a membership triangle. At the three points of the triangle you have yourself (the individual Christian), the whole congregation, and then the pastors or elders. And the New Testament is chock-full of commands and obligations and duties that should characterize the relational lines between any two points of that triangle. It is impossible to imagine how one might fulfill all these commands without what we call church membership.

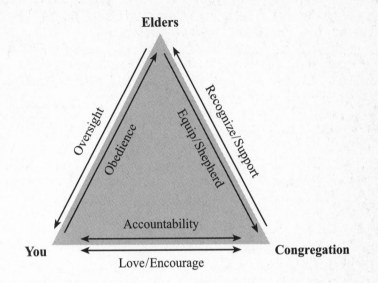

Let's start with the pastors. Hebrews 13:17 says that pastors "keep watch over your souls as those who will give an account." So we pastors will give account to God. But for whom? For all Christians in the world? Certainly no. For all the Christians in a city? No again. Rather, pastors will give an account for the members of their church (see also James 3:1). And that means they will give an account for both particular individuals in the church (see Heb. 13:17) as well as the particular congregation as a whole (Acts 20:28; Eph. 4:11f; 1 Pet. 5:2–3). Pastors have a responsibility to me as an individual Christian, and they have responsibilities to the whole congregation. A faithful pastor looks after both.

The same is true if we stand at another point of the triangle and look toward the other two points. So I, the individual Christian, have a responsibility to obey particular pastors, not to all pastors everywhere (e.g., 1 Thess. 5:12–13; Heb. 13:7, 17). And I have a responsibility to love and encourage a particular congregation of Christians (e.g., Matt. 18:15–17; Rom. 14:19; 2 Cor. 2:6; Heb. 10:22–25; 1 John 1:3–4; cf. John 13:34–35).

Finally, standing at the third point, a particular congregation possesses the responsibility to recognize particular pastors and to support them (e.g., Rom. 10:15; 15:30; 1 Cor. 9:14; Gal. 6:6; Phil. 2:29; 1 Thess 5:12–13; 1 Tim. 4:3; 5:17–20; cf. Matt. 10:10). And it possesses responsibilities to love and encourage me, the individual Christian (e.g., Matt. 18:17; 1 Cor. 5:12).

Every one of these sets of obligations are things you can find in the New Testament. You just might spend an afternoon this weekend reading the book of Acts and trying to fill in that triangle!

A Self-Conscious Commitment

The larger point is, it would be impossible to fulfill quite a few of the New Testament's commands like these without the self-conscious commitment of church membership (see also Phil. 2:8; Rom. 12:3, 16).

The New Testament calls Christians to love one another (1 Cor. 14:1; John 13:34–35). It calls us to examine ourselves and one another (Rev. 3:17; 2 Cor. 13:5; Gal. 5:19–23; 1 John 3:14; 4:1–3, 20–21). It calls us to obey our leaders (1 Thess. 5:12–13; Heb. 13:7, 17; 1 Pet. 5:5). All of this happens not just in a series of relationships with your friends—even pagans have friends—but in local churches. Self-conscious membership is necessary for biblical discipleship, and it gives a specific shape to our discipleship.

So, if we want to fulfill the Great Commission, then normally we must pursue the work of church planting in one form or another. Engendering these kinds of groups of people with these self-conscious commitments is how we make disciples and teach people to obey everything Jesus commanded.

The Commission and the Ordinances

Does the Great Commission envision such a self-conscious commitment? Yes, it does it—to say it once again—through baptism.

What happens in that moment of baptism? Two individuals have to agree that they confess the same Christ, and that one person is joining with another in wearing the Jesus nametag. Notice that there is an implicit affirmation of each other. When we identify ourselves with Christ, we identify ourselves with each other, like two children who belong to the same parents acknowledging that they are siblings.

The Lord's Supper makes this affirmation of one another visible and ongoing. Through the cup and bread we participate in the blood and the one body of Christ (1 Cor. 10:16). "Because there is one loaf," says Paul, "we, who are many, are one body, for we all share the one loaf" (1 Cor. 10:17 NIV). Therefore, we should never "eat and drink without discerning the body of Christ" (11:29 NIV).

Are the ordinances private, mystical experiences? No, they are what the Lord has given us to make our self-conscious commitments to him and to one another.

The Great Commission is not about less than personal evangelism and missions, but it is about more. It is about planting churches where people commit to Christ and to one another as members through baptism and the Lord's Supper.

CHAPTER 7

Four Practices of a Great Commission Church

The Great Commission does not call for churches to act like the Department of Motor Vehicles. Nor does it call for them to act like information booths. These were the conclusions of previous chapters. Now I have one more for you: the Great Commission does not call churches to act like professional sports teams.

The staff of my church likes to make fun of me for not knowing much about sports, which might be fair. But I do know the goal of every sports team is to win the championship. A team will try to hire the best players, build the best training facilities, and optimize its coaching staff all to win its league's top trophy. Sure, a team is glad other teams exist. Without them there would be no league. But its main goal is to beat those other teams.

Now, I doubt very many, if any, churches explicitly think to themselves, "We have to beat those other churches!" But let me ask a couple of diagnostic questions to test for an our-team-is-best mentality:

- Do you happily give away your best players to other churches?
- Do you rejoice if, after praying for revival, revival comes to the church down the street? (Thanks to Andy Johnson for this great question!)
- Do you pray regularly for the church down the street as well as the other churches in your city?

- Do you give any portion of your budget to revitalizing old or raising up new churches in your city, around the nation, or abroad?

Too often, a grotesque competitiveness between churches marks evangelical churches. But a Great Commission church does not compete with other gospel-preaching churches because it knows every gospel-preaching church *is playing for the same team*.

Great Commission Church = Church Planting Church

Here's the broader point: a Great Commission church is an evangelizing and discipling church, but it is also a church-planting and church-revitalizing church. It wants to see the kingdom of God grow through its own ministry, but it also wants to see the kingdom expand beyond its own walls through other churches.

So a Great Commission church is interested in facilitating lots of evangelistic activity going out from itself in order to draw outsiders back to itself. But it is also interested in seeing its efforts culminate in planting or supporting other local churches. It is not satisfied with its own health; it wants to see lots of other healthy, Bible-believing, gospel-preaching congregations.

Such a church encourages other evangelical churches and plants, even if they are several blocks away. And it prays for them by name. It is willing to send out good folks who will help those other churches. It also works to plant or build up other churches on the other side of the world.

A Great Commission church works and prays to raise up men qualified to be elders, and then selflessly sends them out.

It works to align its budget with these Great Commission priorities. Some money is kept for ministry in its own location, but some money is assigned to helping other works, both near and far.

It works to reclaim dying congregations wherever it can.

It works in all sorts of public and private ways to cultivate this team mentality with other gospel-centered churches among its own members. The members and leaders are as happy about a new gospel-preaching church as they are about a new restaurant opening in a land of starvation.

So what does a Great Commission church do? I want to offer five strategic steps—the first four in this chapter, and the fifth in the next.

Cultivate a Culture of Discipling

First, a Great Commission church will cultivate a culture of discipling among its own members. It helps every member own the responsibility for helping other believers grow in the faith. Pastors equip the saints for the work of ministry, says Paul (Eph. 4:11–12), which means the work of the ministry belongs to all the saints. The whole body, speaking the truth in love, grows as it builds itself up, each part doing its work (Eph. 4:15–16; see also 1 Cor. 12; 14).

Disciple*ship* is my following Jesus. Discipl*ing* is me helping someone else follow Jesus (e.g., 2 Tim. 2:2). And in a Great Commission church, *older* men in the faith disciple younger men, and younger women seek out the older women. For instance, if you are a single woman, you might offer a stay-home mother in your church help with the laundry in exchange for the opportunity to ask lots of questions! If you are a lay-elder teaching an adult Sunday school class, you are sure to recruit a junior teacher. And your goal, in a sense, is to train and hand over the teaching job to him. Then you can go and start another class and bring on another junior teacher.

A Great Commission church possesses the geographic sensitivity implied by Jesus' command to "Go." For those who stay, "going" may well mean moving closer to the church or groups of its members. That way it is easy to minister to others throughout the week. Where do you live? Are you helping to cultivate a culture of discipling in your church in where you chose to rent an apartment or purchase a home?

A Great Commission church should be uncomfortable, even pro-vocative, for a nominal Christian. If you show up as such a guest in such a church on Sunday only as part of your casual religious duty, you may not like it very much. You would be welcomed, but its members would not be what you are about. They are about giving their whole lives to follow Jesus, and they commit to help one another follow Jesus. Such a commitment and such activity is part of the very culture: intentional questions, meaningful conversations, prayer, and continual reminders of the gospel.

Take a look at Robert Coleman's *Master Plan of Evangelism,* Colin Marshall and Tony Payne's *The Trellis and the Vine,* or my own *Discipling* for more on this topic.

Cultivate a Culture of Evangelism

Second, a Great Commission church will cultivate a culture of evangelism. On the one hand, members know that the gospel will be preached in every weekly gathering. So they are excited to invite their non-Christian friends. The gospel radiates through the singing, the praying, and every sermon.

Are you confident that any non-Christian you bring to your church will hear the gospel? If not, what can you do about it?

On the other hand, a Great Commission church works to train its members in evangelism, because it knows they will collectively see more non-Christians throughout the week than will ever be able to fit in the church building. So "success" in evangelism is not simply bring-ing your non-Christian friends to church so that they hear the gospel. Success is sharing the gospel with your non-Christian neighbors and friends.

So the church works to equip its members in evangelism so that they know how to share the gospel with others. My own church does this through adult Sunday schools devoted to evangelism. I try to model how to engage with non-Christians in my preaching, particularly in the way I explicitly address non-Christians. We try to equip our members by offering them evangelistic tools like "Two Ways to Live" or resources like "Christianity Explained" or "Christianity Explored." We hand out lots of Greg Gilbert's *Who Is Jesus?* to members for them to give to their non-Christian friends. We also share about evangelistic opportunities through our Sunday evening meeting. Hearing and praying for other members' evangelistic opportunities encourages people's own attempts to spread the good news.

What does the Great Commission mean to you? It means Jesus has called you to be a disciple-maker. He calls you to both evangelize unbelievers and disciple the believers. You should be doing this personally—at home, at work, in your neighborhood, among your friends. You should be doing this in and through your church.

Therefore use your fellow church members to help you. Invite an elder to lunch and ask him for counsel. Share and pray with your small group. Go out and evangelize with your friends.

For more on this topic, look at any book by Mack Stiles, especially *Evangelism: How the Whole Church Speaks of Jesus,* or my book *The Gospel and Personal Evangelism.*

Work to Reach the Unreached Through Missions

A Great Commission church, third, works to reach the unreached through missions. What's the difference between missions and evangelism and church planting at home? Really, missions is just what we call evangelism and church planting when it travels across ethnic, cultural, and typically national boundaries.

Jesus commands us to "go and make disciples of all nations." I have not said much on this topic because so many other books cover this idea so well. But it's hard to know how a church might read this command and not commit itself to taking the gospel to nations that have never heard the gospel before.

No congregation can aim everywhere around the planet. Therefore I think churches are wise to concentrate their own mission efforts on a few places. My own church, for instance, concentrates on several countries in the so-called 10/40 window, which is that region of the Eastern hemisphere between 10 and 40 degrees north of the equator. It's the area of the world where there is the smallest percentage of Christians.

If you are a member of our church, and you express an interest in pursuing missions, we will be able to put more of our resources behind you if you go to one of the locations we already invest in. We are simply unable to sponsor a hundred people going a hundred different places. By that token, we prefer supporting few missionaries with more money rather than lots of missionaries with only a little money. That enables the missionaries we do support to spend less time raising money and more time doing the work of church planting. Plus, it helps us to have a relationship with them and offer accountability.

Our church works with missionaries directly, and we work through missions organizations like the Southern Baptist Convention's International Mission Board. We also work with amazing groups like Access Partners, who helps to place business people in strategic spots around the world in their business vocations, so that they can assist the long-term missionaries on the ground.

What role should you have as an individual Christian helping your church to reach the unreached? Certainly you should pray for your church's missionaries. Get to know them when they are on furlough. Perhaps look into short-term mission trips that will allow you to support the long-term workers. Read missionary biographies. And maybe think about going. We will come back to that question a couple chapters from now.

There is one last thing you and your church can do for reaching the unreached: look for internationals in your own city. My own church works hard at reaching international students, but what international groups live in your city? If you reach them with the gospel right there in your hometown, there's a pretty good chance that the gospel will spread back to where they came from.

Take a look at John Piper's *Let the Nations Be Glad* for more on this topic.

Work to Strengthen Other Churches

Churches commonly have a missions budget line. I think it's worth adding a "Fostering Healthy Churches" budget line as well. Working to strengthen other churches is a fourth practice of Great Commission churches.

My own church uses this line for supporting a number of things, such as our pastoral internship program. We pay twelve guys a year to do an internship with us, most of whom end up pastoring or otherwise serving other churches.

We also use the line to support the ministry of 9Marks, a ministry devoted to building healthy churches.

We intentionally structure our staff so that guys get trained and are sent out. Pastoral assistants serve us for two to three years and are then expected to go. Assistant pastors serve us for three to five years and then go. Only myself and the associate pastors (together with any non-staff pastors or elders) are expected to remain in our church long-term. The rest we equip to go.

Our church sponsors weekend conferences, where pastors from around the world join us for our regularly scheduled meetings as well as several special lecturers and times of Q&A. I also participate in weekly phone calls with several other networks of pastors from around the world for the same purposes. Each one of these conversations gives me the opportunity to pray and work for healthy churches all around the world.

Much of the work we do of strengthening other churches through church planting and church revitalizing we do in our own area, which is the topic of the next chapter. (That whole chapter, in other words, is an extension of this section.) But we do some planting and revitalizing around the world too. For instance, we sent one brother, John, to a church in Dubai, United Arab Emirates, when that church was looking for a pastor almost a decade ago. God has used John in mighty ways to revitalize that international church. One of his key elders, who helped to bring John there, was Mack, an old friend of mine. Once John and Mack got the church to a healthy place, Mack and another brother, Dave, left the church to plant another church thirty minutes away. We also sent a former pastoral assistant and a former intern to help Mack and Dave in that new work. Simultaneously, we sent another former pastoral intern to plant yet another church in another city of UAE.

Now we have three healthy churches up and running in this Muslim country. None of this was a part of some grand plan of ours. In fact, neither the one revitalizing opportunity nor the two planting opportunities were initiated by us. We were just there to pray, help, and send financial and human support where we could. By the way, a number of our members have relocated their jobs to the UAE to help the work of these churches. Our church gains in no particular way other than the sheer joy of seeing God's kingdom expand in this foreign land.

A lot of these examples have focused on what I as the pastor have done. But assuming you are an ordinary church member, what can you do to help strengthen other churches, whether in your area or around the world? Obviously, you can pray for other works personally. You can pray for other works with your family at dinner. You can support other works financially.

Certainly you should be careful about criticizing other churches. Yes, there are places where your church's practices or secondary doctrines might differ from those of other churches. And yes we have deliberate reasons for those areas of disagreement. I am not telling you to throw those disagreements out the window. But keep in mind that those secondary matters over which your church might disagree with other churches are never as important as the gospel we all share. So guard against a critical spirit, and look for ways to rejoice in shared gospel partnerships (see Luke 11:49–50 for Jesus' warning to his overly-narrow disciples).

Finally, recognize that you are either a goer or a sender. So important is this fact that we'll devote chapter 9 to helping think about that question. But first, let's continue the conversation about helping other churches, particularly those in your area, in chapter 8.

One More Practice of a Great Commission Church

I commonly tell my church that we just want people to be spiritually fed; they don't need to eat at our restaurant. There are a number of good places they can go in our city. We simply want the level of spiritual hunger on our planet to be reduced.

A Great Commission church, therefore, looks around to see if there are other churches in its area that can be helped. Maybe they've fallen on hard times. Maybe they have even begun to distort the gospel in their teaching or practice. Whatever the case, we should want to see them reclaimed for Christ. That unhealthy church may well have a bad reputation in its community, giving a black eye to Christianity. A Great Commission church will want to help it recover a good reputation. It doesn't just plant a new church right next to it. It tries to fix what a previous generation of careless Christians left broken.

Or maybe there is a neighborhood in your city, or a far-out suburb, with no gospel-preaching church. It might need a brand new plant. What can your church do to help?

Encourage Gospel Growth Locally

We considered four practices of a Great Commission church in the last chapter. I reserved a separate chapter for a fifth practice not because it is more important than the other four, but because evangelicals talk about it less often. A Great Commission church encourages gospel growth locally.

I am so thankful for what God has done in my own city of Washington over the last two decades. When I arrived just over twenty years ago, there were not many healthy, gospel-preaching churches on Capitol Hill that I would have recommended to someone. Today there are half a dozen just on the Hill I could recommend, and even more throughout the District of Columbia. We list these "sister churches" on our website and on printed cards that hang by our church building doors. If someone doesn't like our church, or the drive is too far, hopefully they will try one of these other congregations.

Yes, we have differences on some things, but we preach the same gospel. We are delighted that God in his grace and kindness has been pouring out his favor on the Hill and on the District. We are in a rich time for the gospel. Is there more to be done? Yes, but thank God for what he has been doing.

God is going to win. Even if your church or mine closes its doors, you never need to be in doubt about that. Paul says, "God's word is not chained" (2 Tim. 2:9 NIV). Keep in mind that Paul had been in prison when he said that. Maybe some of his friends were feeling down about the gospel's advance. Paul replies, "Not to worry. God's Word is not chained. It runs freely. It runs freely even through prisons."

Look at what Christianity has done in Nepal over the last twenty years. Christianity has been illegal in this historically Hindu nation, persecution has been intense, and many Christians have been thrown into prison. But guess what has happened: the Christians in prison began to share the gospel. The prison system became a way for Christians to evangelize the whole country! This kind of thing has happened again and again in the history of God's people. God's Word runs on.

We need to stop being so turfy about our own churches, and look for ways to promote the gospel's advance throughout our cities, including in other churches.

Planting and Revitalizing

A primary way we have sought to promote gospel growth in our area is through revitalizing dying churches and planting new ones.

Revitalizations can be tough. There is a reason that that church has been in decline, and chances are that a couple of those reasons are still members! It takes a particular kind of man to go in and lead a dying church toward health, and the church needs to be in a place where they are ready to receive help.

More than once, such churches have found themselves facing this choice: either they can surrender their building deed and keys to a denominational entity or another church who wants to make them a site, or they can take this offer from us: "we'll give you a number of members, a pastor, two years' worth of salary for the pastor, and you can keep your name and building. We ask for nothing in return. It's all yours." Little do they know that we have been training that pastor to focus hard on the gospel, to preach expositionally, and to love them toward health. Call it a covert op.

Sometimes we have sent men and members to churches in the outskirts of our metropolitan area so that people coming from that distance won't have to drive so far. Sometimes dying churches have become available closer to home. We try to make the most of any opportunity we have for the sake of the gospel.

At the same time, we want to plant new churches in our area. Recently, we sent fifty members just down the road to one of DC's poorer neighborhoods with three of our elders. Thabiti, the lead elder, preached in our pulpit half a dozen times in the six months leading up to the plant. That way, people in our church would learn to trust how he handles the Word and be impelled to follow him. As of this moment, they are meeting in a school and still looking for a more permanent location. And we will do everything we can to help. My guess is that we will send them quite a few more members in the coming years.

The goal in all of this, whether revitalizing or planting, is to see multiple independent witnesses spread throughout the Washington, DC, area, closer to where people live. We want Christians to be able to integrate their personal lives and church more easily, going back to last chapter's discussion of cultivating a culture of discipling.

Prayer, Ministerial Fellowship, Core Seminars, and More

There are a number of other things we do to encourage gospel growth in our area. Weekly we pray in our main gathering for other churches by name. We also partner with those churches for evangelism in different ways, such as lunchtime talks in the business community. We also invite pastors of other churches to attend our prayer meetings to share how we can pray for their churches.

I started something called the Columbia Baptist Minister's Association, where I get Southern Baptist ministers in the area together. On the first Tuesday of each month we meet to fellowship, to counsel one another, and to pray. How strengthening and encouraging it is to hear about other gospel works in our city!

Over the last few years, several young church planters have shown up in Washington, DC, and come to us for help. When we can, we love to help. If a guy manages to earn our trust, we'll even send him members and supply preachers when he needs a break. Our hope is that a number of other churches in our area see us as a resource for them, one who asks little to nothing from them, but has plenty of love and care to give.

Lots of people leave our church due to the transient nature of life in Washington. I knew when I moved here that loving this congregation would be like hugging a parade. This can be difficult emotionally. But it is also a wonderful opportunity, and we try to capitalize on this transience. For example, we turned our traditional adult Sunday school program into 13-week, topic-driven "Core Seminar" classes.

We asked ourselves, assuming we have a person for two to four years, what's all the content for the Christian life we want to put in his or her backpack? What should basic training include? For that reason, we offer classes on the basics of the faith, a short evangelism class, a longer evangelism class, Bible overviews, church history, systematic theology, biblical theology, how to read the Bible, spiritual disciplines, guidance, courtship and marriage, parenthood, finances, fear of man, apologetics, Christians in government, manhood and womanhood, and more. All this is our way of both strengthening our members for their own sakes, but also equipping them for whatever churches they go to next.

If someone works his or her way through the entire curriculum, we encourage that person to grab someone else and use it as a way to disciple him or her.

And You?

Again, some of the examples above feature what I have done as a pastor. But the Bible teaches that the entire membership finally has responsibility for the gospel ministry of a church. That means you will play some role in helping your church to catch the vision for encouraging gospel growth locally.

One very practical issue is how you should think through whether to stay in your present church, go with a local plant or revitalizing project, or even move overseas. Many Christians make their decisions about whether or not to move in terms of what is good for their education, job, or family situation. They even make decisions based on the weather, the commute, the lifestyle, their hobbies, and pleasures.

If that's you, I want to challenge you to submit your life decisions to Jesus' Great Commission command. Commit your whole life—whatever you have left—to fulfilling the call to make disciples, teaching them to obey everything he has commanded. When you come to making these kinds of major life decisions, if you are able, settle on a church first, and then sort out other matters of job, house, schools.

Are you a high school senior trying to figure out where to go to college? Make a list of half a dozen great churches in the country. *Then* ask yourself what colleges are in those cities.

Are you a businessman? Does your company have offices overseas? Are you aware of churches or missions work that could use your help in any of the cities where your company has offices? Might you suggest a transfer?

Are you a retiree? How and where will you spend these years?

A Great Commission mind-set will change the way you think about life's big decisions. And that brings us to the next chapter.

CHAPTER 9

Should You Stay or Go?

In order to fulfill the Great Commission, the first disciples *went*. But they weren't perpetually leaving and going.

Sometimes young Christians hear the command to "go" and treat it like the basic command of the Christian life. That's a fairly short-sighted way to think. Once you go, you have to stay. If you're always going, nothing will ever get done except the accumulation of more frequent flyer miles. In order for the *go* to have any meaning, you need to *stay* for a significant amount of time—a few weeks, a few years, maybe the rest of a life.

The question that every Christian faces is, should I move to where the gospel is not now known to be a part of a church-planting team there? *Or* should I join a team that either plants a new church or helps to recover a church nearby? *Or* should I stay in my present church, worshiping and discipling and evangelizing while supporting others who go out?

All three options can be good. They depend on who you are and on what the Lord is calling you to do.

Twelve Factors to Consider

I want to suggest twelve factors for you to consider when deciding whether to stay in your present church or move to another local or international congregation. You should consider:

49

1. **The purpose of your move.** If you are thinking about leaving, would your purpose be largely negative—to leave because of something you don't like in your present church? Or would your purpose be largely positive—to build up a gospel work elsewhere? If you go, it should ideally be for positive reasons. Moreover, you should not leave based on a sense of guilt or false ideals about what a "mature" Christian would do. Negative purposes, misplaced guilt, and false ideals will not sustain you through the challenges of supporting a new or revitalizing work.

2. **The theology and philosophy of ministry.** Does the church or planting team you are considering believe and teach God's Word correctly? Do they have a biblical understanding of both the gospel and what a church is?

3. **Evangelism.** Is the church one to which you can bring your non-Christian friends because you know they will hear the gospel, and will they see the gospel faithfully lived out? (Obviously, this may not be the case in a revitalizing project, at least in the beginning.)

4. **Edification.** It is right for you to want to grow as a Christian. Therefore, you should work to be at a church that helps you to grow spiritually. Are you prospering in your present church? Do you think you would prosper at the other? Would leaving be spiritually damaging to you, or to someone else? Think of how the flight attendants on an airplane tell you to put the mask over your own face before placing it over the face of the person traveling with you. In the same way, it is okay for you to care for your own spiritual health first. You need to be able to breathe and grow spiritually if you want to help others.

There are three different categories of people in the church: the unhappy people, the people who are doing just fine, and the people who are growing like crazy. The unhappy people generally should not join a church planting or revitalizing team. Now, in full confession, my *temptation* as a pastor is to send precisely these people! But that's not wise. If you are unhappy in your present church, it's probably better for you to stay among the people who know you well and can help you work on the causes of that unhappiness. Besides, you just might take the unhappiness with you to the new church that needs your help.

If you belong to the third group—you are presently growing like crazy—you, too, may want to stay in your present church for a while. You're growing! Don't stop what you're doing! Now, if this growth has endured for some time, perhaps talk to an elder and think through the matter together.

The best people to join a plant or revitalizing project are often people from the middle group. This is most people in a church, after all. If that's you, you are doing fine. You're growing, but slowly, nothing exceptional. You are stable and can be a real help to a new work. It might even give you a little jolt!

5. **The strategic nature of the church's work.** Is this a work that seems particularly important, to which you would like to contribute and feel that you can? Is there a strategic God-given vocational opportunity that would afford opportunities to support a particular church, particularly overseas? Is there a people group that you want to reach with the gospel?

6. **The ministry you presently have in your church.** Consider the ministry God has given you already, and be very careful about leaving if a particular ministry depends on you. Perhaps your teaching or discipling skills are being put to good use already, or perhaps you could put them to better use in a start-up. Maybe you form relationships quickly and that would transplant well into a new location. Or maybe it takes you a long time to form relationships such that you may want to think a little more before moving. If you're not a "net exporter" of ministry in your present church—in evangelizing, discipling, encouraging— there's little reason to think you would be in another church.

7. **The particular pastors you would be supporting.** You may have a personal relationship with a man or his family. Or maybe you have found yourself growing in a marked way under his teaching. Those are good reasons to go and support the work, and what a wonderful encouragement you could be to the leaders and others!

8. **Geography.** How far do you presently live from where your church meets and most of its members live? Does your proximity lend itself to regular attendance, easy volunteering, and folding your life in with the lives of other members? How does where you live impact the evangelistic ministry you have in your neighbors' lives, or in the lives of your work colleagues? If you live far away, might you be used to establish or encourage a good work closer to where you live? If you live close, I might discourage you from joining a new project unless you are willing to move to wherever the new project is happening.

9. **Life stage.** Your life stage is a legitimate thing to think about. Are you single? Do you want to find a spouse who agrees with you theologically and practically in your understanding of the Christian life? If you are a father, will the prospective church be a good place for you to disciple your wife and children?

10. **The state of your finances.** Again, it is completely legitimate for you to consider if you cannot afford your present situation, or any possible future situations. Will you be able to afford rent? Education for your children? Other living expenses? Paul observes that "if anyone does not provide for . . . his own household, he has denied the faith and is worse than an unbeliever" (1 Tim 5:8). On the other hand, have you considered whether you really need everything that you've assumed you needed? Be careful about your assumptions.

11. **The state of your relationships with others.** You should leave a place when your relationships are in good shape, not bad shape. You should not leave in order to avoid dealing with hard relational issues.

12. **Prayer.** Do you think that God would have you go to another church or to stay in your present church? We have freedom in Christ. There is often more than one good choice in front of us. Praise God for the freedom we have.

Some Should Go, Some Should Stay

Just because a move might be costly doesn't mean you should not go. It has been costly for most of the saints who obeyed Jesus' command to go. And unless you live in Jerusalem, praise God that someone paid that cost and took the gospel to your nation and your city and your house so that you believe!

Is the point of this chapter to say that some of you should leave your churches? Kind of. Some should go to help struggling churches. Some should plant new ones. Some should go overseas. And some should stay.

Of course people have to stay for any given congregation to remain a congregation. Every church needs consistency in leadership, discipling, and long-term friendships. In fact, staying in our culture is often the countercultural thing to do, especially among the younger generation. With all the career or educational transitions that characterize modern urban life, the radical thing to do for some will be to stay in one place for decades.

Whatever you do, don't make such decisions rashly. And don't make such decisions in isolation, but make them in prayer and conversation with your friends who know you well, and with at least one elder who knows you.

CHAPTER 10

The Grand Goal of the Great Commission

The grand goal of the Great Commission is the glory of God in the church.

If Jesus is the image of the invisible God, how do we see Jesus today? Jesus is not to be worshiped through physical icons or images. We have no account of him teaching his disciples to draw or sketch or sculpt. We have the books they wrote, but no images they made for our adoration.

Instead, Jesus has created a people for his very own through the preached Word. In the church we discover the blessing of the visibility of the character of God. In the church we see what God is like. We know we will see him ultimately when we see his face (see 1 John 3:1–3; Rev. 22:4). But now, in the local church, all the nations should witness the display of the glory of God's goodness and love, and so bring him praise.

Christ identifies himself with local churches. The church is his body. He is its head. His power should be on display in our churches. They should reflect his manifold wisdom. They should make the gospel visible. Churches are his evangelism plan. They are where his kingdom authority is exercised.

The local church is where disciples are made. It is where these disciples are baptized in the name of the Father and of the Son and of the Holy Spirit. It is where Christians are taught to obey everything Christ commanded. And for these glorious ends, Christ has promised us his Spirit and authority until he returns.

Church planting is the normal business of the local church. The Great Commission is normally fulfilled through church planting. I pray you give your life and church to it.

Notes

1. P. T. O'Brien, *Consumed by Passion* (Lancer, 1993), 45.
2. Ibid., 42.

SUBJECT INDEX